D1555830

Meditations Through the Year

Meditations through the year

Nature's Cycle of the Seasons in Guided Visualisations

Dorothea Breitzter–Kings

ASHGROVE PRESS, BATH

First published in Great Britain by
ASHGROVE PRESS LIMITED
4 Brassmill Centre, Brassmill Lane
Bath BA1 3JN
and distributed in the USA by
Avery Publishing Group Inc.
120 Old Broadway
Garden City Park
New York 11040

ISBN 1–85398–029–3

First published 1992

Photoset in 12/13½ pt Sabon by
Ann Buchan (Typesetters), Middlesex
Printed and bound in Great Britain by
Bookcraft, Midsomer Norton, Avon

Contents

Meditations Through the Year

Introduction

This collection of reflective meditations through the yearly cycle of the seasons has been inspired by a deep communion with nature. From the bright awakening of blossoms in springtime, the hope of all good things to come, it moves to the splendid fast fleeting glory of summer, a celebration of life, light and energy; then to the culmination of nature's bounty in the gifts of harvest, and the magnificent 'Grand Finale' of autumn leaves in bright shades of gold, copper and red, before the cycle turns towards the approaching silence of frost and snow. Then winter, the season of rest and sleep, within which, at the darkest hour, the light is reborn to grow and lead again into a new cycle of awakening. . .

The journey through the year in nature is full of powerful images. We can see them as symbolic states which live, I feel, in each of us because we are part of nature. Not just does our life in its stages reflect the yearly cycle, but every phase and chapter in our life awakens, blossoms, culminates, bears fruit, and then it wanes again into silence out of which, in its own time, new inspiration and fresh impulses are born. The cyclical laws that are at work in nature without also govern nature within.

In former times when life was slower and more obviously dependant on our natural environment we found it easier to live in touch with nature's cycles on the outside as well as within ourselves. Many activities in daily life, for most people, were directly related to the seasons, and a good instinctive attunement to living with nature was important for survival.

Today we enjoy modern comforts that, to a large extent, shelter us from the extremes of seasonal conditions and allow us to pursue our chosen activities in an ongoing way, particularly in the cities. We can also, up to a point, prolong the stages of spring and summer in our lives, deferring the ageing process with the help of diet, health and fitness programmes, beauty products and even plastic surgery!

Our increasing knowledge and inventions have 'liberated' us from many of the limitations that nature once imposed on us. But has this independent modern lifestyle not also dissociated us from ourselves?

Today, many of us have to spend a large part of our time in highly unnatural environments that can cause stresses and tensions we are often not even fully aware of. Many popular foods are so highly processed that the balance of natural goodness has been lost. They often contain unnatural additives, or come to us from far-off places that are climatically and environmentally extremely different and unrelated to those in which we live and eat. Allergic reactions, irritations and illnesses which can prove hard to diagnose have been on the increase during the last decades. Our culture is so extremely oriented towards youthfulness that the rich gifts of maturity are undervalued. Most of us see in the natural process of ageing only a threat to still being able to enjoy life to its full. Death is a taboo area in our society; we have no vision of a spring to follow our winter.

Pure water, natural food and clean air have to be consciously protected and worked for these days, and we have globally arrived at a point where the life and well-being of our abundant green earth is severely endangered. Often we talk about protecting nature as something outside ourselves. Perhaps we still do not fully recognize that by protecting nature we protect ourselves. Our survival is directly dependent on nature's survival because WE ARE A PART OF NATURE!

For each of us to help respect and care for nature we can work on getting more in touch with it, learning to feel and understand it more intimately, opening up to the experience of this wonderful life energy within and without us which flows through all of creation. Attuning ourselves to nature can be very healing. It can put us in touch with that great underlying oneness that our planet shares with all its amazingly diverse plantlife and creatures. It can open us to love: for ourselves, for others, for this beautiful planet as a whole and so work against the painful isolation that afflicts many of us today. It can help to start us off on the path to becoming more healthy, if we want to, both physically and psychologically.

If we take some time to slow down enough to get in touch with nature and its cycles we will at the same time harmonize and tune ourselves. The following exercises were created out of a sincere need for balance and peace of mind. I would like to share them with you, because they have helped me tremendously in times of tension and distress, and I have found them enjoyable and centering at easier times, too. Their form has borrowed from Yoga relaxation techniques and the guided visualisations of Transpersonal Psychology and Psychosynthesis, while their content has been directly inspired by the deep experience of the life of nature through the seasons. By tuning into the cycles of that pulsating, ever self-renewing, inconceivably eternal life energy we can draw closer, and learn to touch, the self-renewing, the immortal within ourself.

Before You Start

It is quite easy to do the following exercises on your own. You could choose the one that fits the time of year and make it a 'theme' for the month or read through any one that feels right for you at the time, getting into the spirit of it and then take up a relaxed position and spend some time visualizing. What matters is that you get the feel of the theme, even if you do not remember all the details.

On the other hand it can be very nice having a friend guiding you through a visualization, reading it out to you slowly, or you could even read it out for yourself onto a tape which you can then play any time you feel like it. If you do, make sure you leave sufficient space between the instructions to give yourself time to visualize fully and without feeling rushed.

You can do a visualizing meditation whenever you feel like it and wherever you feel comfortable, indoors or out in nature itself, and little preparation is needed. It is important, however, that the time you have set aside for it remains undisturbed by outer influences. Choose a place and time where you can be pretty sure that you will not be interrupted.

Now take a comfortable position in which your spine is straight and your muscles can relax. If you can, stretch out fully on the floor, making sure your back is straight. Close your eyes, breathe evenly and allow yourself to turn inward, letting go of the outside. Slowly let the sounds fade into the distance, so that all you remain aware of is the gentle ebb and flow of your breath. Concentrate on it for a little while, and when you feel calm and focused enough you can begin the visualization.

For those occasions when you might feel the need for a really deep relaxation I include the following general relaxation exercise, which has two parts. Such an exercise can be used on its own to relax body and mind from stress, and to help you feel centred and composed. It is a useful device for working on an inner letting-go of situations and compulsive preoccupations. Conversely, it can also help you gather, focus and centre body, mind and feelings before approaching a task that demands concentration. It serves as a helpful start to the visualizations, enabling the body to relax and mind and feelings to quieten, so that concentration can increase and your imagination can flow unhindered by physical or mental tensions. It is important, though, that enough time is available, so that the exercise is not done in a rushed going-through-the-motion style, and so that if the mind should wander, you will have enough time to let yourself gently come back to it, and carry on from there.

After a few experiments you will have a fair idea of how long you need. You can then, according to the time available, choose either to do part one only, or the entire exercise. The beneficial result depends much on your ability to let yourself enjoy the relaxation, forgetting about pressure, and allowing a sense of wellbeing to grow in its own good time.

General Relaxation Exercise Part 1

This is a variation of an ancient Yoga exercise called Savasana, or 'corpse pose', which is used fully to relax the body and free it from all tension, so that it can be left to rest for a while without needing attention. The mind becomes calm and able to focus in, and the whole being is quietened and harmonized by the gentle, steady flow of breath.

For this exercise it is best to lie on the floor rather than on a settee or a mattress, for it enables you to straighten your spine better, and to open your chest and lie with your whole body in a straight line. Put a mat or blanket down to insulate you from the cold, and wear warm, soft, loose-fitting clothes or take another blanket to cover you. Choose a reasonably quiet, well-ventilated (yet not draughty) spot. If indoors, switch off electric lights and other buzzing electrical appliances nearby that might disturb you. It is best not to try the exercises straight after eating, for a full stomach might make you drowsy and does not help concentration. Most important, though, is that you approach relaxing with a cheerful and positive attitude, so that you allow it to work for you and make you feel comfortable.

Lie flat on your back on your blanket on the floor and have a good stretch. Stretch out your legs right up to the heels as well as the toes. Stretch your arms sideways and feel your spine elongate. For a moment, while stretching, tense your muscles, clench your fists, even screw up your face, then breath out fully and let all stress go. Now rest comfortably with your body lying straight, and your arms pointing out at a soft angle from your torso, palms facing up, fingers relaxed. Your whole body lies passive now, safely supported by the firm ground.

Let your breath become soft and even, without forcing it, let it quieten into a steady rhythm and observe it for a while. Let it guide you inward.

Now direct your attention to your toes. Visualize all tension seeping out of them, down into the ground and away, until they are fully relaxed. Let your feet become soft, as if they were expanding in a pleasant warm bath: the balls of your feet, the insteps, the heels . . . all stress is being absorbed by the ground they are resting on. Let go of the control in your ankles, they can rest now and be passive. Picture to yourself how this relaxation lubricates the creaky joints.

Now turn to your legs: release them from the strain of standing and walking. Let your calf-muscles become soft and heavy . . . and your knees rest passively, well supported by the floor . . . now let go of those strong thigh-muscles, let them spread soft and floppy onto the ground they are resting on, they will not have to work for a little while. Feel how both your legs are soft and heavy now, and all tension has gone from them.

Relax the muscles in your bottom and let your abdomen become soft. Your bowels and organs rest lightly in their right positions; all pressure and stress seeps off them now, down and away through the good earth where tension is in time transformed again into positive energy. Gently, your abdomen rises and falls to the natural rhythm of your breathing. Let go of your control over your stomach muscles until your whole tummy feels relaxed and soft. Your digestive system quietly keeps on working by itself; it knows what it has to do, you just give it the freedom and space to get on with it.

Observe your ribs softly contracting and expanding to the even rhythm of your breathing. Your lungs expel the used air to take in the fresh and new. Visualize how the oxygen revitalizes and cleanses your bloodstream. Your heart beats in time. It pumps your blood in a regular flow through your entire body, so that the refreshing oxygen is carried to every part of it as healing, loving messages sent from your heart.

Now visualize the tension draining from your shoulders. Allow them to rest comfortably and evenly on the floor while your chest is able to expand and open freely. Let go of the muscles in your arms: the upper arms, then the elbows, then the lower arms; let them become soft and warm and heavy. Your hands, too, can lie soft and loose now, with fingers relaxed, in their natural, lightly curved position, a bit like a bunch of bananas.

Soften your neck, let it rest easy, as a straight continuation of your spine. Slightly move your jaw and tongue, unclenching your teeth, then let them find their naturally relaxed position. Let your lips and the muscles around your mouth become soft. Feel the soft flow of air going in and out through your nostrils as you breathe. Let your nose relax.

Now feel your eyes resting underneath closed eyelids, gently tucked in as if under soft, warm, heavy coverlets. The eyes are always so active and prone to holding tension, but now they do not have to work at seeing forms and translating colours. Now they can be soft and passive, and rest looking inward, securely contained in their sockets beneath the protective, gentle cover of the closed lids.

Let your ears simply hang by the sides of your head; they do not need to pay attention to the sounds from outside for now. Feel your face muscles become softer and softer, let gravity smooth out all those little wrinkles. The skin on your forehead and around your skull can relax now. Every hair on your head becomes soft, lies down and relaxes.

Unclench your brain, let it soften and rest on its protective enclosure, and take a little time to feel any remaining tension sink down and out through the back of your head, and away into the earth beneath.

You are now fully relaxed. Your whole body feels soft, heavy and warm. Your head is cool and bathed in soft light. You are at peace.

General Relaxation Exercise Part 2

Now you are free to be a little point of light at the centre; like a little flame breathing and burning steadily in its own space. You have come back to that quiet place inside yourself where you can be entirely at peace, where you do not want or need anything, because everything is here in potential, in essence, yet nothing is actual, nothing is cluttered by things, thoughts or feelings.

A complete, empty space, yet full of all you need simply to be a small point of light, breathing and burning steadily. You have come home again to this quiet centre inside yourself, which is always there for you if you relax and slow down enough to find it. Take some time to feel this homecoming, to enjoy this peace, and rest in the little point of light, breathing softly.

Then, when you feel ready, turn your attention towards the urge that makes you want to return back to your daily life. Even if you feel this urge to be reluctant and clouded by doubt and apprehension, try to tune into your will to live which comes straight from the source. Let it radiate out from the centre, slowly filling you with life and energy. Feel how, here at the source, the will to live has not yet been complicated by condition, it is just a simple urge towards the light, a will to experience and explore the adventure of living . . . in your body, in the world. . . Let yourself feel and explore this urge, and then visualize that you are given a gift by your own centre to help you meet the challenges your life will present.

The gift is gentle perseverance, a stability of positive mood that will help you get from day to day one step at a time. It is not like the harsh force of willpower, but gentle, loving and allowing: an accepting attitude, a willingness to integrate all the facts of your life; taking it steady while keeping a positive outlook on the whole, open to seeing creative possibilities. It is the gift of knowing you can carry on with your life and cope. Allow it in fully, imagine it flowing through every vein and into every muscle. Let it fill your body with new strength.

When you are ready open your eyes and take a few seconds to adjust. Then turn over onto your right side and lie comfortably for a little while, and then do the same on your left side until you feel fully ready to get up.

March

Spring Equinox, New Beginnings

Imagine yourself on a day out in a large, old, beautifully land-scaped park. It is the time of the spring equinox, light is increasing again and day and night are equal in length now. A tingling, exciting surge of energy starts to be felt in the atmosphere: spring crackles in the air even if it has not fully sprung yet. The wind is still cool, but when it brushes your face there is a freshness and sweetness in it that leaves you in no doubt that winter is turning at last.

Open yourself to this stirring sensation . . . let yourself tune into the arousing energy of approaching spring, along with all of nature around you . . . Now the sun comes out from behind a passing cloud: it is surprisingly warm and strong. The first rays of spring sunshine: remember how you have longed for them on dark, overcast winter days . . . They are heaven's kiss of life to the earth after the long winter sleep. Enjoy how good they feel. Along with all the growing things around you let yourself, too, be kissed into a spring awakening by the first warm sunshine.

Everywhere the sap is rising in the trees. Only a short while ago the trees stood dark and frozen, now suddenly you can see new life budding on every branch. Each twig stretches out hard little tips towards the sun. They will get fuller and softer with every day now, until at last they will open up and give birth to tiny, tender young leaves. Here and there, in sheltered places, you come upon a tree or two already clothed in fresh spring green. Delicately shaped little leaves unfold like tiny fans from their burst buds. They have been ripening in their protective shells for many cold, dark days, waiting for light and warmth . . . and now they are ready to come out, sensitive and young, the promise of a lush, green summer stretching ahead.

Now imagine that walking on ahead you come to a cluster of fruit trees, already in blossom, standing in a sheltered dip between gently rising slopes. It is a magnificent sight: soft, billowing clouds all white and pink, made up of millions of delicate, silky, perfectly-shaped miniature blooms that drip abundantly from every branch. See how the sun lights them up, how every petal responds with a silky shimmer. They wave and waft in the wind, and even though they do not exude a strong flowerlike scent they fill the air with fresh, moist sweetness. Breathe in deeply . . . let it fill you with the pure, sweet quality of blossoming spring. Let it refresh and revive you . . . in body and spirit.

As you draw nearer you hear the silvery sound of bells, followed by the sweet, soft blowing of clear trumpets and horns . . . Listen . . . it is a fanfare to herald and welcome spring. And then you see that the ground of the orchard is covered with early spring flowers. There are still some snowdrops, and here and there a crocus shines rich and purple in the sun. Pale yellow primroses huddle together in groups, their little bells jingling and chiming in the breeze; while the first of the daffodils, in bigger clusters blow their trumpets with the joy they feel at the coming of spring. Open your heart to the music . . . join in with the celebration . . .

At the far end of the blossoming plantation the walk continues amongst more budding oaks, birches and beeches. Soon you come across an old tree stump where a mighty tree must have fallen many years before. Only the very bottom part is left, and the wear and tear of many seasons has helped to rot that huge body of dead wood into a fascinating labyrinth of cavities. Take a little time to look at what highly imaginative and varied shapes even the forces of decay and disintegration in nature can produce. The yearly layers of wood stand rugged and broken like rings of old teeth, crumbling more every year and changing into a brown, fertile humus that goes back into the earth to enrich it. Out of the centre of this old tree stump a young sapling is growing . . . from a seed that must have had the good fortune to take root in this highly fertile spot. You can see it is a baby birch, and it is doing very well in this sheltered position. Its tender green leaves are already opening and you watch them flickering with sunlight as they quiver in the wind.

Take a little time to consider this small tree. It knows how to pick up energy from outgrown material, from old and waning form and use it creatively to continue into a new cycle.

In our lives, similarly, we cannot undo what has been, but the background of the experiences we have had and the lessons we have learned forms a rich and fertile humus into which new seeds for our future can be planted. Sometimes life does it for us, quite naturally: when the time is right a new seed blows in on a wind of change and takes root in our life. At other times we need to choose to do the planting. Spring is the time of new beginnings. If you feel the need for a fresh start in any aspect of your life, let the surge of spring energy all around inspire and encourage you. . . Let go of the drowsiness, inertia and defensiveness of the winter that has been. Along with all of nature budding everywhere, try to open yourself towards a new cycle of growth, and like the little birch that grows in the old tree stump let new life grow to new heights out of the outgrown forms of the past. . .

April

The Flower

Imagine yourself walking in a spacious garden lit by clear spring sunshine. You can feel the warmth of the sun on your face, feel it loosening your limbs which are still stiff from the long cold winter. Spring has fully arrived now. There is a strength and warmth in that sunshine that you had almost forgotten; it has the power to awaken all living things from the cold, dormant states of winter and inspire them to new life and growth. It feels such a relief. All around you in this garden you can sense a corresponding yearning for the awakening touch of the sun, and together with all the other growing things you turn towards the sunshine and enjoy bathing in its warmth, willing to let go of stiffness and defensiveness.

The garden you are walking in is large and well designed. There are terraced flower beds facing the sun, with steps between the levels. At the bottom, a huge weeping willow, just turning green, droops gracefully over a small pond. You can see the glowing red shapes of goldfish moving slowly in the cold grey water beneath the rippling pattern of waves made by a little fountain that fills the air with a cool, fresh mist. Everything is getting ready for the season of warmth and light to come, opening out and striving towards increase. Growth and unfoldment will happen fast now, and the overwhelming beauty of spring is like a joyful celebration that marks the beginning of the season of increase. Have a good look around, and enjoy the colourful splendour. . . Fruit trees stand along the edges of the flowerbeds, bulging with blossom; rich, full, pink ornamental cherry-trees, and white ones like brides in full wedding dress, apple trees with their sweet, sensitive white blossoms blushing rosy red, and the tall pear tree enveloped as if in a gown of cream-coloured lace. Even the knobbly old magnolia tree is beginning to burst the swollen, velvety brown hoods that cover its fragrant, pinkish-white petals; soon they will open like cups, longing to be filled with spring sunshine.

Look how the sun lights up the flowers, too. The terraces look as if they are boiling over with the riotous wealth of colour. After the pale, mute tones of winter this luminous magnificence still seems miraculous. There are thick clusters of primroses in bright red, purple, yellow and white, all with a shiny yellow star at their centre. There is a whole sea of pansies in white, yellow, rust, salmon and purple, their dear little faces shimmering with a rich, velvet-like texture that makes their strong colour look even more intense. There are daffodils, narcissi and the first tulips, all lit up with a silky sheen, and there are purplish-blue, pink and white hyacinths exuding an intoxicating sweet scent. You can see many other budding plants that need just that little bit more sun before they, too, will be ready to show their blooms.

Let your heart open to the beauty all around. . . Now imagine that you find yourself a comfortable spot in the sunshine, close to one of the flowerbeds, where you sit down, relax, and let yourself forget about time. . .

Right in front of you a tender green shoot pushes its little head out of the cool dark earth towards the sunlight. You watch as it slowly straightens itself up and sprouts two tiny leaves at either side of its stem. See how sensitive and young this little shoot looks; and yet it is full of inner strength and determination to grow. It stretches up a bit more, unfolds more leaves that turn towards the sun, and now you notice that at its top a tiny bud is swelling steadily. You can watch it getting bigger as the plant slowly reaches its full height.

Now the little bud, too, turns towards the sun. Warmth and light envelop it and you can watch as it changes colour and increasingly bulges with a round ripeness until, suddenly, the sepals part and you witness the unfolding of a beautiful flower. . . Slowly each petal opens and stretches out its creases until it is all smooth, silky and perfect. Give yourself some time to enjoy the lovely face of this flower. . . The sun lights up the strong, yet subtle colour; the soft, organic texture glows with a silky sheen and irridesence in the lovely spring light. Its form is a masterpiece of harmony and balance, and even the small, unpredictable-seeming imperfections add to its live and growing uniqueness..

Feel how it radiates a moist freshness, gives off a gentle fragrance. Breathe in, enjoy, and let it draw you closer to the flower. . .

At its centre you find the stamen symetrically arranged and full of pollen. Here the light is coloured as the sun shines through the flower petals as through a cathedral window of stained glass, and the air is fresh and sweet with the taste of honey. Imagine how the bee feels . . . let the centre attract you, too. Slowly let yourself go into the richness and fullness, let yourself merge with the colour, the softness, the freshness, the scent, the taste . . . right into the very core, the heart of the flower.

Now you find yourself back in that familiar place, still and quiet, where you are free to be a little point of light breathing softly, secure in its own space, centred and at the centre, resting peacefully in contentment. There is no need for anything, not even thinking and feeling, there is simply being and breathing. . . If thoughts come, gently let them go again and return to the soft ebb and flow of your breath. There is no hurry here at the centre, just give yourself time, let go of life's pressures and concerns and allow yourself to forget. . .

Here in your very own space at the centre you can rest and let

your energy renew itself . . . Take as much time as you need. . .

And then, when you feel ready, try to tune into a feeling of strength welling up from the depth of the centre into this fertile state of relaxed quietness and peace of mind . . . it is the strength of a renewed will to live, of feeling refreshed and rejuvenated, and of turning once more towards life with an open, youthful sense of eagerness like that of the young plant that grows and bears its flower turning towards the sun.

Imagine the gentle but powerful energy which caused the plant to grow, welling up from the depth and rippling through you in soft, refreshing currents that strengthen you and give you heart. Then you feel yourself rising lightly on one of these energy waves, like a bead of sap being drawn up through the stem of the flower into its sweetly scented, blossoming face. And from there you can step out into the sunlight, as the bee would, and maybe bring some of the freshness, the sweetness, the colour and beauty into the garden, and even beyond . . . into your life.

May

The Clearing

Imagine yourself lying on a stretch of dry, sunwarmed grass in a little clearing in the woods in May. The sun is shining softly and steadily, everything on this still day is warm and slightly steamy. The powerful energy of growth pulsates all around you and you can feel the moist lushness of spring warming towards summer . . . a nursery to all growing things. The trees are clothed in tender new leaves of May green. The skeletal structure of bare branches you could see all winter lies hidden now beneath the juicy green foliage that gives a freshness to the warm day.

Let your eyes explore the little clearing. . . It is surrounded by great wild rhododendron shrubs bursting with uncounted clusters of trumpet-shaped blooms . . . a sea of purple flames. Deep violets, rich purples and shades of magenta cascade in showers of blossoms from tree height down to the green ground. Look at a fully open cluster . . . a purple flowering globe of perfection. See how in each flower trumpet the slender stamen lick up towards the sun. See the richly spotted leopard pattern spreading from the centre out along a path of silky purple petal. . . All these globes of purple flowers are lit by the sunshine, so that the light around you in the clearing has a slightly violet tint, and the air is fresh and sweet with the moisture and scent of living petals.

Now listen to the sound of life all around. . . Birds are singing. Clear, sweet voices rise in song from high in the trees, some nearer, some more distant. Listen to the joy and the force of life there is in bird song. Notice the concentrated energy in their angry territorial calls, or in the noisy cries of passing jays and magpies. They all live intensely in the here and now.

There are other sounds, too. Squirrels hurrying up and down trees scratch the bark with their claws and dash noisily along the branches. Sometimes you can hear a vole or a mouse rustling for a second in thick undergrowth, or the loud squeak of a shrew defending its territory from a rival. Try to feel the energy and purpose of these warm, furry little creatures. Feel how intensely they live every minute of this warm spring day, how so totally immersed in it they are.

And as you lie still and listen you become aware of a continuous droning sound, barely audible at first, but as you tune in it seems to get louder. You are becoming aware all around you of myriads of busy insects and the humming made by their countless little wings as they beat the still air.

Here is a bumble bee. Dizzy on rhododendron nectar it buzzes about in its soft, tiger-striped fur coat, with wings as pretty as an Art Nouveau design in leaded glass. See how fine these wings are, how transparent, and how the sunlight breaks through them into rainbow colours. Watch it bumble from flower to flower, stuck all over with pollen, which it gathers into delicate pockets on its legs. This little bee, too, lives so intensely on this balmy day.

There are many other insects around . . . some are flying, some making their way slowly along a blade of grass, clad in colourful, shining armour like the knights of old. Some can jump unpredictably high, others stalk about skilfully, always managing to place six or eight delicate long legs in the right places. They all are busy and full of life, yet none of them is in a rush. They all move gracefully at their own pace, they all have time. . .

Take a little time to experience even more fully the nurturing qualities of this lovely warm day . . . let it loosen you up, enliven you with spring power, and draw you out as it does the flora and fauna. Tune into the abundant energy all around you, energy that manifests in such a multitude of delightful and diverse forms. Plants and trees, birds, mammals and insects are all now living to their full capacity. They are naturally at one with the seasons and have abandoned themselves to this time of activity, warmth and light.

See if you, too, can feel some of this trust, this openness to the good things in life. Try to let go a little, loosen the defensive, constricting old attitudes and fears. Along with all the living things around you open up to the approaching summer and say 'yes' to life. . . Let your own energy join the heightened flow of nature, and welcome in the joyful season of abundance . . . in nature as well as in your daily life. . .

June

Summer Solstice, Festival of Light

Imagine yourself walking along the shores of a beautiful clear lake out in the country. It is a fine sunny day and the time of the summer solstice: the longest day of the year. The sun shines pleasantly warm and a mild wind moves across the water and rustles in the leaves. The air you breathe is fresh and clean, and as you walk through this spacious landscape your step is pleasantly light and you can feel your heart opening to let in the clear, bright beauty of this summer day.

Take some time to notice the quality of nature around you, a quality that is so characteristic of this time of year. . . It seems that suddenly every weed and plant has grown huge and lush, where a very short time ago they were only tiny. Everywhere you look nature is bubbling and boiling over with rampant growth, and you can see delightful shades of tender, young green which are so special to this time of early summer.

The leaves are nearly all fully grown now, yet still they are soft and supple and have a light, fresh colour; summer sunshine has not yet hardened and darkened them. Watch how they quiver as soft gusts of warm wind ripple through them. See how the light reflects back from their shiny surfaces, and how their undersides flicker silver in the sunshine.

This is a time of rising sap and intense growth. Rainwater is sucked up fast by trees and plants all sprouting and greening. Herbs and wild flowers open their buds to the long hours of daylight and nature fills the soft green grasses with rich seeds. This is also a time when many old wounds are being healed. Light and warmth now penetrate into the darkest crevices and touch them with life. New growth covers up the old scars that were so visible during the cold season, and you can see new shoots sprouting and unfolding everywhere, promising a green future. All around you life is winning.

Listen, there is birdsong everywhere. The first batch of baby birds has hatched now, but they are not yet fully grown. They have all summer ahead of them to become ever more skilful at flying and finding food for themselves; all summer to outgrow their soft baby plumage. The birds are very busy now, they wake up early with the sun and stay up late in the evenings. There is so much to do and the long days make it possible.

Everywhere around you the animal kingdom is at its height of activity. They are all reproducing, all bringing up families: in the treetops, in the undergrowth, down in warrens under the earth and even in the waters of the lake. Whether they are furry, feathered, or clinking about in horn tissue armour, they all are out and busy, animated by the light and warmth.

Take a look around. . . In the pastures you can see sheep, cows and horses getting frisky on their diet of fresh, juicy grass and the abundance of daylight. Young rabbits, too hungry to wait for the cover of darkness, come out while the sun is still out to nibble at the grass here and there . . . and for a moment you can catch a glimpse of a tiny spider, almost transparent, floating by on a gossamer . . . riding a soft summer current to connect anew and spin on wherever the wind cares to take her. Did you see the sunlight break into bright rainbow colours in the tiny, translucent thread?

In northern lattitudes the sun does not go down at all now and Midsummer's day is celebrated as the festival of light and life. This is the culmination of energy in nature, the height of the victory of light over dark, day over night, life over death, growth over stagnation.

In many ancient cultures the longest day was celebrated as one of the most important festivals of the year. Light has always been valued as the prerequisite for life and energy on this planet, and loved as a symbol of clarity, understanding and spirit.

Turn towards the lake and look into the distance. A small white cloud momentarily covers the sun and you can see its

shadow move across the water. Then suddenly the cloud passes and bright sunlight bursts free, lighting up your view and filling the whole landscape with a glowing, pulsating radiance. The light of the sky is reflected in the water, creating a tremendous sense of luminous space and freedom. Let your heart open up to this joyful vision. . . Keep breathing in a naturally soft, even rhythm, and on every in-breath be conscious of taking in that pure clear light. Let it fill your lungs and from there spread out through your entire body, permeating every part of you, right up to the boundary of your skin . . . cleaning, energising, revitalising and healing. If there is pain and sickness in any part of you, visualize this part especially being bathed and strengthened by the clean, pure light. Let some of the joyous space and freedom enter into you through your in-breath. Then, when you breathe out, visualize how impurities, tensions, negative emotions, restrictive feelings, sicknesses and fears leave your body on each exhalation. Watch them disperse and dissolve in the vast, luminous sky. Then, on the next in-breath, let the clear light fill you in their stead. . . Breathe on softly and evenly for a while, until you feel lighter at heart and in your body.

And when you turn away from the lake and walk back into the landscape of your daily life you can, perhaps, illumine it with some of the light, the energy and the spaciousness that fill you now. . .

July

The Oak

Imagine yourself walking through healthy woodland on a fine summer's day. Dappled sunlight dances in ever changing patterns on grassy spaces between the trees where ferns, herbs and wildflowers grow in green abundance. You walk on into a spacious, airy glade where many oak trees stand and where there is plenty of room between the tree trunks for you to move about freely and with ease.

A variety of birds are singing from up in the leafy branches, and you can sense the many wild little creatures in the undergrowth, even though they may be hiding from your sight. Oak forests allow for such an abundance of life: oaks are very hospitable trees. One tree can provide a habitat for hundreds of different types of plants, insects and animals in a long life that is likely to span several centuries.

As you look around you, notice that each of the oaks is at a different stage of its life. There are small, tender young shoots growing together in clusters, of which only one or two will, in time, grow to full height. There are strong, straight, youthful trees, asserting their space with branches stretched out on all sides. Their bark is even, their posture tall and upward, and they look towards the future, towards new centuries to come. Then there are old oaks which, although still strong and powerful, have lost the upward motion in their stature and have increased in girth instead. Their bark has become rough and tatty, mosses and ferns grow up on the rainfacing side, and where their heavy branches part, clusters of bracken thrive, high up in fertile hollows. These old oaks look full of character: each one a distinct individual, expressing a particular quality in the way it stands. Some of the very old ones look strangely whimsical, as if they have carried on growing on one side only, forgetting about the other; or they may have largely died off and now stretch out one last living branch, looking like St Christopher carrying the child. Hundreds of summers and winters have brought out the uniqueness in each one of them, just as experience of life unfolds potential and character in us.

Now let yourself feel attracted to one oak that particularly appeals to you. Imagine yourself lying down comfortably on soft pads of moss beneath it, closing your eyes and tuning into the qualities that this tree expresses. . .

Imagine . . . it all starts with a little acorn. Having dropped onto the fertile early autumn soil it lies there brimming with ripeness and potential until a squirrel, or maybe a passing jay, finds it and buries it for winter provision. Then, in the dark earth, processed and softened by rain and changing weather, bitten by frost, it cracks open one day and tentatively sends out a tiny root that burrows deep into the cold earth, groping for support. When nature awakens again in spring a slender shoot appears above ground, bearing its first hard little bud towards the light and warmth that is increasing now with every day. Two tiny leaves unfold, tender and almost transparent, while at the same time the root thickens and grips firmly into the earth. Once established, the little tree makes steady progress, adapting well to the cycle of the seasons. At first it grows amongst a number of sibling trees that support each other in wind and weather, but in time most of them get eaten by rabbits, blown over or left behind in growth. An oak requires a great deal of space to grow to its full stature, and only a chosen few can succeed.

Imagine what it feels like to be a young oak destined to survive, establishing lasting support far into the earth, growing and stretching straight towards the light, the future . . . more powerful and solid with every new year. Become this beautiful tree in your imagination, feel the firm support in your roots, feel your strong young branches purposefully stretching out and your crown unfolding.

What a relationship you have with the earth. What a relationship you have with the sky. Seasons come and go, winds and storms tear at your branches you keep growing towards the sun that greens your leaves, you rejoice in the rain that washes them clean.

Take a little while to feel what it is like to have so much time, a long, slow life, spanning centuries. There is no rush and there are no goals to reach. You just grow steadily, unfolding yourself at your own pace, accepting what life brings to you.

As the years go by you reach full height and now you start to thicken up and grow into a shape that is a physical expression of your personal uniqueness. With each new ring that swells your trunk you become more full of character, distinct from the others around you . . . you are growing into a real individual. . .

Many birds come to nest in your branches and peck out the insects that live in your bark. Squirrels chase each other up and down your trunk and feast on your acorns, while rabbits dig amongst your roots, building their warrens; and tiny mice rustle amongst the fern and ivy that climb up on you. Countless little creatures come and go, new generations with every year; their lives are lived so much faster than yours. You have met and known them all, and have provided a habitat for each one, allowing them to live their little lives in your shelter. Myriads of insects, too, live in your bark, drill into your acorns or lay their eggs on your leaves. Fungi grow amongst your roots and bulge out from your trunk, their subtle network of minute threads clinging to your very fibres. Wildflowers and ferns thrive in the shady patches beneath your branches, fed by the compost your fallen leaves provide.

You are big and powerful, you can graciously accept these passing forms of life depending on your unwavering support. They are all part of the cycle of waxing and waning.

Slowly, over the centuries, while you are growing ever more individual, you will find that the expansive power and strength of your youth has faded. You are an eccentric old oak now, wide in girth and very knobbly. You cannot feel some of your branches any longer, and parts of your wood are rotting and weak. Yet this, too, you can accept with good grace; you have had so long and rich a life and have held out so strongly for centuries . . . it feels a relief now to get by on less energy, for less needs to be channelled into those parts of you that are still green and growing. And as long as they are, you will have the strength to carry on, from season to season, with the same solid dedication to living, and to producing fine acorns, of which a chosen few may well grow into strong trees like you to secure a green future for centuries to come.

Spend a little more time feeling the rooted strength and stability of the oak in your own being. Let it inspire you with the confidence to spread out and live to the full, trusting in your potential and individuality, letting it unfold naturally at its own pace, and accepting what life brings, as the tree does.

Let it inspire you with the strength to carry on, one day at a time, adapting to the seasons of life . . . and to offer the fruits of your efforts, generously like the oak does, so that a chosen few, perhaps, may take root, sprout and grow far beyond . . . into a fertile future. . .

August

The Holiday

Imagine you have the chance to take some time off from the regular rhythms of your life. The days are bright and warm, and to celebrate the outdoor season of summer you decide to go on a holiday. All the demands of your daily life, which have been a burden for too long, all your deadlines, commitments, responsibilities to the people around you, your duties, tasks and regular chores can be left behind now for a while: you are going to escape!

Think of them, one by one, and feel yourself getting lighter as their weight drops off you and they slip into the background.

Here, too, is your chance to get a break from the people in your life, from those you find irksome and even from those whom you love. Think of them and imagine saying 'good-bye' for a little while . . . you will see them all again soon enough. Feel yourself stepping out of the rut . . . out into freedom . . . lightly and without a care.

Where will you go for your holiday? Picture to yourself the wild open landscapes you have so often dreamt of and wondered about, where nature is fertile and abundant, where there is so much space to get away from it all . . . and then choose from among them one which you really fancy. Imagine yourself setting out on the journey, with your daily life left safely behind until your return. Turn your mind away from your cares, and towards the open potential of making discoveries, the excitement of new experiences . . . now you are giving yourself the time and space to explore new grounds.

Maybe inside yourself there is a part which has never been able to find much expression in your daily life, a part of yourself that does not quite fit into life as you live it. Like a separate person inside you this part may want and need other environments, other activities and maybe also other company than that your life usually provides.

Take some time to tune into your inner world and let this special part of you emerge and take on form. . . It could appear to you as a person from your inner world, male or female, or maybe as a symbolic animal or even a magical being. It is a part of you which is now being given the chance to express itself in symbolic form, enabling it to communicate with you. Turn towards it with goodwill and the intention to invite it to come along on holiday with you.

What does this inner part of you look like? How does it move and behave? In what symbolic appearance has it chosen to show itself to you? Perhaps you have met with this inner figure before and you are old friends. But even if you have not and find this character strange and not altogether acceptable, approach it with kindness and goodwill and try to communicate. Remember, it has not had much attention and has been living in the dark. To be taken on your holiday might do it a great deal of good. Ask it what it most wants from you? What does it need from life to be well and happy? Maybe on this holiday you can allow this inner part of you more room to live in your life.

Imagine ways in which this could be done: you could let it choose some of the places you are going to, do some of the activities it enjoys doing, even wear some of the clothes it likes to see you in, and allow it to choose some of the acquaintances you will make on your trip. You could let it lead you into new experiences. This inner character may be able to show you aspects of life which you will never see in your regular routine. Together you could turn this holiday into an interesting adventure.

Now imagine yourself at your holiday destination. Take a while to look around and notice how different it is from the environment you are usually in. You have wanted to come here

for a long time and now you are here. Relax and enjoy it, you can feel at peace here.

What is it you like about this place?

What are the qualities that have attracted you here?

What can you do here that you cannot do at home?

Who can you be here that you cannot usually be?

If you feel any new impulses, give yourself time to experience and explore. Are there any qualities that you would like to develop and include in your life? A change of environment can inspire a sense of freedom to branch out into something new and to make fresh discoveries, in the outer as well as in the inner world.

Now turn again to the part of you which you have brought with you on this holiday. Is this inner character contented here? You might like to ask it to help show you the way to new discoveries and experiences and promise it some space for expression in your life in return.

Take the opportunity to enjoy and explore freely what it is like to be a little different from how you have always felt you needed to be. Tune into the spirit of exploration; let the change of environment on the outside stimulate you to discover more about the lie of the land in your inner world now that you have the time. Maybe, with the help of this other part of you, you might gain a new and larger sense of integrity and bring a richer, fuller you back from the holiday into your daily life. . .

September

Autumn Equinox , Time of Abundance

Imagine yourself sitting comfortably among the moss-padded roots in the lap of a great tree in your favourite country park. Summer is gently drifting into autumn . . . day and night are equal in length now, but the sun is still warm and the sky is clear and blue. The leaves are drying up now, and here and there you can see them already changing colour: splashes of yellow, copper-tone and rust spread out among the faded green. But the day is still warm, mellow and a little drowsy, a 'fare-well' gift of passing summer. All is quiet about you as you rest under the big tree, and you feel like losing all sense of time on this unhurried, dreamy, golden day. . .

Now and then the silence is broken by the sound of acorns rattling through the leaves and falling to the ground. Have a look at the different types of trees standing nearby. All are heavy with ripe fruit: the oak with its thousands of acorns sitting tightly in their cups, the beech with its tiny triangular nuts, and the old horse chestnut tree with its big, dark chestnuts, shiny like polished mahagony, bursting out of their spiky shells.

Each fruit is a new tree in potential, but most of them end up as winter food for the creatures of the forest. As you look around you can see many other kinds of fruit-bearing trees . . . small, dry looking ones bursting with showers of bright red or orange berries, the knarled old wood looking aflame with ripe life, and the tall, dark fir trees and pines dripping elegantly with symetrically patterned cones. In the gardens and orchards, too, the gifts of autumn are ready: sweet, soft plums drop to the ground, green apples hold out their red cheeks to the last ripening sunshine and yellow ones hang glowing like golden globes. Bulging pears swing heavy on the creaking branches, and clusters of brown nuts adorn the sturdy hazel bushes. . .

Now and then you notice a squirrel gathering its harvest, collecting acorns or beech nuts and digging them into the ground, probably never to be found again. But in this way, while gathering for themselves, they also help the cycle of nature as they plant, like little gardeners, the seeds which in the spring may sprout new shoots. The birds, also, while revelling in the abundance of bright berries are helping to spread seeds simply by letting their droppings fall. Nature is already preparing for a new beginning while still delighting in the culmination and the fruits of this present passing cycle. . .

All nature's energy, from the awakening in early spring and the bursting into blossoms to the greening and growing all through the warm summer months is now culminating in this harvest . . . a time of celebration and plenty. Nature's work has been completed for this year: blossoming, growing, ripening . . . and now the fruits are offered in this time of generous abundance . . . the 'grand finalé' of the cycle. From now on, light and warmth will retreat so that nature can relax, slow down and drift into cold, dark forgetfulness to rest and sleep and renew the energy . . . until spring comes again, awakening all to fresh vitality.

Take a little while to consider the marvellous abundance that exists on this planet, our fertile earth, and all the many diverse forms of life it supports: mountains and forests, wilderness, fields and gardens . . . springs, rivers, lakes and vast oceans . . . all working together in an amazingly complex system to maintain nature's balance. Each landscape supports its own particular flora and fauna and has its own distinct character and beauty. And every form of life contributes to the larger whole in its own special way.

How open are we truly in our hearts to nature's generous abundance? How easily do we take it for granted and only ask for more, forgetting to look at what is already there, to appreciate the wonderful gifts of this earth?

Nature is so unselfish, so generous. Look at the trees around you: they have grown and ripened their fruits all summer to let them go now for the greater good. They do not count their cost; for a little sunshine and rain they will do the same again, year after year, working and creating according to their basic essence. Then they offer the fruits of their labour and rest for a season, before starting all over again. . .

Take another look at the rich autumnal scene that surrounds you. Among the many different trees you discover a small, slender apple tree with big, round, juicy apples hanging heavily from its branches. Their cheeks glow rosy in the sunshine as they softly swing in the breeze. This little tree is offering its apples to you and all others who come.

Take a little time to open your heart and let this picture of abundance in. Make a point to look more for the richness and beauty in life, and to appreciate the gifts that our green planet provides. Many old cultures used the apple as a symbol for nature's gifts of plenty, and you might like to take such a symbolic apple from the little tree with you when you are ready to return to your daily life, to remind you of nature's generosity and abundance that is so freely given and will continue to sustain our life on this planet, if we only co-operate and look after our earth in return. . .

October

The Well

Imagine yourself walking into a fertile little valley, sheltered on either side by two gently sloping round hills. In the hollow dip between nestles a well cared-for garden, glowing in autumn colours. You come up to the wrought iron gate and walk in. Here, sheltered from the autumn winds, bloom many of the last flowers of this year. The sun shines softly, with a clear, liquid light and you see shrubs and bushes lit up as if aflame with brilliant colour, their radiant leaves and bright berries shining out in warm tones against the clear blue sky. It is a beautiful day, but getting late in the year; autumn is well on its way now. Dry leaves float to the ground, their edges curled up and rusty in colour. Together they spread a many-textured carpet over the soft, faded grass. The last ripe fruits, too, are ready to drop from the trees. Look around, you can see various kinds of apple, pear, hawthorn and walnut trees, all glowing with ripe fruit and autumn splendour.

You notice how well tended and healthy everything is here: plants and flowers are particularly large and rich in colour, and you can feel a sense of quiet strength and well-being permeate the whole garden. . . Give yourself time to look and tune into the magical atmosphere and the timeless peace of this special place. . . Enjoy the beauty and serenity, and the soothing presence of so many growing things. . .

Then, as you wander on, you come to the lowest lying spot in the centre of the garden. Here, sheltered in a circular depression and surrounded by flowers, lies the source of all this fertility: an ancient well, covered by a heavy, round lid, beautifully worked in wrought iron and wood.

Bend down and lift the lid . . . and look into the deep, dark, cold waters of this ancient well. . .

A cool, slow, timeless feeling rises from the depths underground. You can feel an eternal quality, an utter steadiness and deep resourcefulness that causes these waters of fertility to flow in an unceasing, even rhythm up and out from the bowels of the earth. Here is a centre for the gift of life and plenty; even in times of severe drought this well has never been known to fail. Fed by an underground spring of clean, rich, sparkling mineral water that has been purified deep in the earth before being pushed out towards the light, it bestows on all who come and drink a draft of

purity and cool refreshment. . .This is an elixir of life.

Let yourself be attracted to the crystal beauty of the water, and the promise of healing and renewal that you can sense coming from it. Take some into your cupped hands and then, slowly, drink of the water of life . . . internalise its cool, steady strength and let it become part of you. . .

Rest a while comfortably among the flowers on the soft, grassy slopes by the side of the well and feel the cool water refresh and revive you. Slowly, let its cool, healing glow reach all the parts of your body, particularly those that have been unwell or uncomfortable, and feel how it eases and soothes them. You have drunk of a healing well . . . allow the water to renew your energy and help heal your hurts. Allow it to wash and cleanse you . . . body, mind and soul.

Imagine the water of life also soothing your mind . . . let it wash over old, outdated thought patterns that have become restricting, soothe away worries, thoughts of bitterness and negativity . . . and refresh your tired mind to new, insightful and creative thinking. Feel how subtle and clear the effect of the water is.

And now let the elixir of life also reach your heart. Imagine it washing away hurt, pain and resentment, and smooth over your feelings of weariness. Feel the sparkling crystal waters bubble inside you with new energy, uplifting your mood like prickling champagne, rekindling your spirit and reinforcing your will to live. Let them inspire you to live more fully, more from the heart.

Give yourself enough time to enjoy the purifying water reaching and renewing every part of you, really feel yourself becoming lighter and filled with new energy.

Then listen out for a note: imagine that you can hear a steady, pleasantly deep humming sound, unobtrusive and mellow but always there, vibrating gently. It is the sound of the well, the sound of energy and resourcefulness steadily welling up from unknown depths and spilling over in generous abundance into the light of day; the unceasing gift of ever renewing life for all to share.

And as you listen to the steady humming note you can feel its vibration gently tingle in your body . . . you become aware that the sound is both within and without, that you hum with life yourself and vibrate with resourcefulness welling up from unknown depths . . . that you, too, are a well of energy whose fertile waters of life can help to heal others and create beautiful gardens with colourful flowers, leafy plants, and trees full of fruit . . . if you let them spill out into the light as a generous gift to all.

November

The Stream

Imagine a golden day in late autumn. Winter will be coming soon, and these are the last trailing days of a lovely, long autumn. It is still warm in the sunshine, and all around the last righ shades of rust, copper, yellow and gold seem luminous in the light. You are walking along a wild little stream out in the countryside. The clear water ripples swiftly past you, it is clean and fresh and cool, and you can see right through to the bottom of the little riverbed where it washes over rounded stones and mosses. Occasionally you catch sight of a fish jumping and splashing, or glinting in the sunlight as it darts away in the shimmering water.

Summer's lush greens have turned autumn-coloured every-where. Along the stream the banks are still richly overgrown with grasses, herbs, and a few last wildflowers. The roots of trees and bushes spread out along the banks right into the water. They all draw life and nourishment from its never failing supplies, while they in turn provide the habitat for countless small creatures living by the water's edge. Picture the many different birds that come every year to spend the summer here, and the ducks and geese drifting and paddling, or the graceful dragonfly on a summer's day, hovering still, with wings that reflect the sunlight in brilliant shades of blue, green and gold. Imagine the water voles sleeping in their holes in the river banks, and the tall heron that might well come here hoping to catch them as they paddle by.

Now you come to a beautiful big tree. Its roots, too, extend along the bank right into the water; its mighty golden crown provides an area of dappled light and shade on the ground below. It is still warm enough to stretch out comfortably in the shelter of this big and lovely tree. Lie down on the grass and relax, while the drying leaves above you softly rustle and you can hear the sound of the stream murmuring, ever changing, by your side.

Listen to its melody for a while, and let yourself forget about time. Let the fresh, clear, sparkling water attract you, and while your body rests safely in the lap of the big tree, let your soul draw nearer to it, touch it, then slowly slide in to bathe in it. . . Feel how the glistening ripples refresh and soothe you; let yourself merge with them until you can feel yourself part of the current, dissolve into the joyful splashing motion over wet rocks glistening in the sunshine . . . light as a gas bubble prickling in champagne.

Now you are a tiny drop of water, whole and complete in itself, yet part of the stream which has sprung from a rock high up in the far hills and flows down all the way to the sea.

Explore how it feels to be so liquid, so supple, so fluid. . . Sometimes you roll over round, mossy stones on the bottom, at other times you sparkle in the sunlight while you ride the ripples of the surface. You can bend and stretch into any shape, and no obstruction can harm or hinder you: you simply let your shape adjust to flow around and past it.

Here comes a tiny fish: it swims right through you. A little tickle, and you gently part yourself to let it pass and then merge back into a whole.

Here comes a big fish: it opens its mouth . . . and gobbles you up. Now you are in the dark. But then it opens its gills and you escape again into the light. You are so fluid and adjustable that nothing can hurt or threaten you.

There are many just like you in the stream together, all having adventures of their own along the way. Some get sucked up by the roots of trees and bushes that dip into the river, and they then travel on along the fine veins inside the tree and help it to grow. Some will get expelled again as a fine mist from shiny green leaves. Others splash onto hot rocks and evaporate in the sunshine before they rise and join the passing clouds. A few have even soaked into the bread that someone threw to the ducks and now have to wait in a dark belly until they are passed out again. But drops of water do not need to fear: their strength is in their subtlety, their ability to adjust . . . They are indestructible.

As the stream flows on there are ever more of you travelling together. Other streams merge with yours and it becomes a large, slow-moving river, made up of many multi-millions of water drops. But, aothough you all tend to push and shuffle along a bit, you get on well together, you are so akin. Ever slower you move along in this large company, until at last you come to the sea.

Here you are taken in by a vast, even rhythm, swaying you slowly back . . . forth . . . back . . . forth . . ., it is like being part of a very large organism breathing steadily. See the waves rolling up and crashing noisily onto the shore: millions of little water drops recklessly riding the white foam and jumping to land. . . Further out at sea you can feel the pull of the rhythm quieten. You can see fish, much larger than those you met in the river, and watch shy seals diving for them, or maybe you will even see a whale, huge and powerful, and in the distance . . . was it really a mermaid that you saw swimming swiftly away?

But it can be rather dark in the big sea, and you feel attracted upwards, towards the surface, pulled to ride the white foam in the sunshine. There is so much space: the sea below and the vast sky above. Enjoy the sense of freedom as you let yourself drift along: a little drop of water on the surface of the sea. As the sunshine winks in you, you reflect all the colours of the prism.

You feel yourself getting quite warm now, and your attention turns to the sky. Slowly you let the sunshine evaporate you into a fine mist. Now you feel yourself rising up, light as a feather, to join the fluffy white clouds sailing on the wind. . . Far below you can still see the ocean, but you are floating back towards the land. Feel how light you are, how easy it is to move as soft mist. Enjoy . . . let yourself drift a bit. . .

Now you begin to see land again far below. Other clouds join your company, and there is quite a throng. Your cloud turns heavier and darker and sinks a little in height with the weight of all this gathering mist. Down below it seems the trees are calling out to you, the land wants and welcomes you. And as your cloud steers towards the high hills you can feel the air cool, feel yourself contracting . . . and before you know it you have changed back into water, and suddenly you feel so heavy you could drop. . .

Let go, let yourself fall, towards the land that is calling out for you to come home. Light and fluid you drip onto the ground and slip striaght through its surface with ease. Now you are in the dark earth, your progress is slow, but steady. Let yourself respond to the pull of gravity. Feel how it carries you down, you do not have to work or struggle, just let yourself sink. . . Soon you join up again with other drops, running through narrow channels inside the hill. They pull you along, all pressing upwards together, and you can feel a longing to see daylight again and know that it is not far away. A small opening appears at the end of a tunnel, and together you make towards it; it seems the earth itself is helping you to push on ahead. The light increases and suddenly you gush out into it, light and free, and find yourself once again bubbling down a little stream . . . skipping over stones, sliding down waterfalls and sparkling in the sun.

Then you come to the place where your body lies safe and comfortable under the beautiful big tree, and there you leave the water and reunite with it. And as you feel yourself lying on the green grass you can still remember the subtlety, fluidity and lightness you experienced on your journey as a drop of water. You can still feel the strength and confidence that comes with the ability to adjust to changing situations and to ride lightly on the crest of waves, and you know you can take some of this ability as a gift back into your daily life. . .

December

Winter Solstice, Rebirth of Light

Imagine going out for a walk on the shortest day of the year: the day of the winter solstice. The hours of daylight are few, the sun rises late and sets early, leaving the mornings dark and the evenings long. The mid-day hours of light feel quite precious and pass all too quickly.

It is a fine, clear, crisp winter day. As you step outside you feel the chill air touching your face . . . going in through your nose . . . and into your lungs . . ., brisk and invigorating. And when you breathe out, the air from your lungs is moist and warm and comes out as a soft white mist. After a while you realize it is milder than you thought it was at first. Relax into a comfortable walking pace that keeps your body warm and supple, and enjoy the great space of cool, clean, fresh air through which you are walking. Let it enliven and revive you.

The ground on which you step is lightly frozen in parts: brittle sheets of ice stretch out over small dark puddles, and myriads of shapely crystals cling glistening to sticks and grasses.

Take a while to look more closely at the magnificient variety of frozen form along a blade of grass. . . See the sunlight break on the ice into bright rainbow colours. This, too, like blossoms, flowers and fruit, is part of the transient beauty of the seasons' cycle; perfect for a short time, then changing again with the rhythm of nature.

Some parts of the ground are not yet frozen and rather soggy: stretches of heavy mud on the paths and waterlogged lawns. It rains a lot at this time of year, but the trees and plants are not active and growing now, their roots do not suck up much water. Puddles lie about waiting to be absorbed by the cold earth, or slowly turning to ice.

Beneath the frozen surface, thought, there is still some warmth and life: imagine all the animals hibernating in their warrens . . . There are tiny mice in their holes, and soft furry rabbits, stoats, weasels, even badgers, and many others, sleeping the winter away, all huddled together for warmth and wrapped in a dream . . . until spring comes with the first warm sunshine to wake them up again. Many kinds of insects lie encapsulated in the ground in a state of deep unconsciousness. The seeds of autumn's fruits, too, are all dug in under the surface, being processed by the waters and frosts of winter until they are ready to sprout with life in spring.

As you walk on, try to feel the quality that is so special to this time of year: there seems to be more space; cool, empty, hollow space, and in it there lives an echo. Nature is so quiet and still, and sounds carry further now that all is asleep. Listen . . . can you hear them amplified by the echo of winter?

The sun never rises high in the sky now. See how it lights up the tree trunks from a low angle, casting long, slanting shadows. There is a blackness to those shadows you do not find at other times of the year; patches of black that the soft light cannot dispel hide underneath branches, among treetops, in shrubs and hollows, and behind stones. Cold silent shadow creeps over the landscape, subtly and quickly, when the sun goes down.

You can see the patterns in the tree bark standing out starkly in the silvery light, and the graceful skeleton shapes of trees reaching up into the dusky sky. See how each one is individual, unique.

Enjoy looking far: your vision is not restricted now by leaves and plant life. Beyond the sleeping bones of trees and bushes you can let your sight expand far into the silent countryside. Now and then the quiet is interrupted by some winter birds pecking about in the cold, wet ground, or a waking squirrel searching for a store of nuts before it goes back to its bed.

For you, too, it will soon be time to turn back towards the warm indoors. Before you do, though, look ahead into the distance where you can see the sun turning red and sinking towards a hilltop crowned with trees. . . This is the shortest day

of the year; when this sun rises again tomorrow it will shine that little bit longer, and then longer again each day, until light will overcome darkness and nature awakens again to a budding spring.

This was held to be a sacred time in many ancient traditions: the rebirth of the light. The energy is turning again from waning to waxing, from dying to growing, from dark to light. Celebrations were held by many old cultures, with candles, symbolic fires and feasting to help draw the sun back on to a new cycle of increase.

As you watch the fiery red globe slowly sink behind the black trees on the hill, imagine that you, too, can help draw the sun back; you too, can consciously partake in the change of the energy tides.

Let it inspire you to make a deliberate choice to let go of darkness and to look towards light . . . in yourself, in your life. Make a choice to try to release your attention from negativity, fear, hate, frustration and sadness, and to give it to appreciation instead, and to hope, beauty, joy and love.

Allow the light to increase, on the inside as it does on the outside, so that your life can grow into a new cycle, towards a new spring.

January

The Fortress

Imagine yourself walking up a slope towards an ancient fortress that circles the hilltop like a crown. It is one of these soft, still winter days when cold mists cover the valleys with the icy lustre. As you climb higher up the hill you leave the mist behind, the view gets better with every step, and soon you can see for miles all around. Fine wispy skeletons of trees reach up from frosty landscapes that lie bathed in pale light, the thin, soft, watery sunlight of a winter's day. You are ascending out of the sleepy, misty valley, and you can see the castle walls towering on the hilltop above you. Your path winds on towards the big main gate. The last few steps seem steep . . . but now you are getting level with it.

You walk across the heavy wooden drawbridge, over the moat, between the two guard towers, and now you enter the almost circular walk between the guarded castle and the many turrets and battlements of the strong outer wall that hugs the hilltop.

Much of this walk is covered with grass and you can stroll about and explore freely. Take you time to look around and enjoy the remarkable old architecture: towers and arches, walls and battlements, protruding balconies, small turrets and pointed rooftops, tiny winding passages and secret stairways beckoning you to the hidden places of the past. Feel how the rambling charm of the building pulls you layer upon layer into the hidden places of the past. Everything has been entirely made by hand and only natural materials have been used. You can feel the quality of a time when daily life was more organic and crafts grew directly out of the resources found in nature.

Touch the crumbling old stones: you can feel where the sun has warmed them even on this winter day. Feel their slow, steady quality: solid, ancient, enduring . . . outside the limitations that time imposes on your life. Imagine their enormous lifespan, their beginning in an obscure past when heat and pressure fashioned the shapes of this earth. When the substances of our young planet were yet unsettled, intense heat and force were churning up matter everywhere, and where the pressure was the greatest, the hardest of our stone was formed.

This stone is very hard. It has endured many centuries and will endure many more. It took generations to build this fortress with it, and generations to live in it. It has seen times of peace and times of war, times of plenty and of need, deeds of courage, valour, generosity as well as of injustice and treachery. It has seen events of joy and of sorrow, and known so many people who have lived and died inside its walls. And while it witnessed the changing times it has remained unchanged itself: it is still the reliable, strong, solid stone it has been for thousands of years . . . only older, still, and richer.

Stone absorbs vibrations as it absorbs the warmth of the sun and the wet of the rain. Ancient stones feel very special; they have a venerable quality. They have witnessed life's epxeriences through the centuries, and they have absorbed them all, yet they have not been broken, they are still standing strong, the same solid old stones, only enriched by the passing of time. . .

Take a while to feel this quiet, ancient, rich quality; enjoy its comforting strength and solidity. . . This is the insight of the mystic who sometimes wears a round stone bead as a symbol of the spirit. The round bead stands for wholeness, completeness in itself, while stone, symbolic of the permanent spirit, outlasts experiences and transient form. And while it absorbs qualities and matures in richness it remains unchanged in its essence, reliable in its permanence.

Now try to imagine that you have this quality of the symbolic round stone inside your own being. . . feel its strength and permanence in your very core, your centre. It is the strength to go through life and digest experiences without being damaged, to remain essentially the same, yourself, while absorbing, maturing

and growing in stature through meeting the challenges and learning the lessons that life presents. It is the ability to live in the world of transient form without losing touch with the eternal, the spirit, and to transform experiences into a richness of understanding and lasting wisdom. . .

Take some time to feel and explore this strength, this inner stability inside yourself, and then, when you are ready, walk back down the hill still keeping an awareness of it, back out into the misty valleys of life.

Febuary

The Sea

Imagine a clear, dry morning. Winter is loosing its grip on the land, and you can begin faintly to sense that spring is just beyond the horizon. You decide to take a walk along a sandy beach. The air is cool, fresh and stimulating, you can feel how it clears your head and invigorates your senses: you feel awake and very alive. The pale morning is full of subtle colours, but crisp and still unworn. You walk towards a group of smooth white rocks where you find a comfortable little spot to sit down and rest, sheltered from the wind, and looking out to sea.

The distinct, savoury smell of salt and seaweed comes across to you in whiffs, now stronger, now fainter . . . you had almost forgotten that very characteristic smell of a sea-breeze, but now that you are here you recognize it at once. A taste, too, goes with it. You lick your lips and find a faintly salty, savoury taste: the taste of the sea.

Your skin tingles in the fresh, salty morning breeze, and the sand beneath you feels fine and soft every time you move, yet pleasantly crunchy, also. The smooth white rocks which shelter you have been washed by waves in the course of countless years into soft and rounded shapes. It feels good to rest against them and to smoothe your hands over their gentle, even surfaces. . .

Let your eyesight rejoice in roaming the distance. So often your eyes are tired and strained, confined by having to look at objects in close focus. Now you can let them explore the far horizon, where the vast body of water meets with the endless sky above, and yet extends much further still . . . beyond the curb of the earth and away, out of your vision.

See the seabirds circling high above; here you can do the same in your mind, all around is freedom and space. You can feel the wind blowing in from the water; playfully it ruffles the fine dry sand. Wind just like this has been blowing over beaches for uncounted centuries, and just like this it will keep blowing far into the unmeasured future. Long before you were here, long after you will have gone . . . let it help you let go of pressure and open yourself to a vast rhythm and spaciousness that goes far beyond our ordinary awareness of time.

And all the while, there is the sound of the sea . . . waves lapping against the shore in a slow rhythm, uneven but steady. Listen to the peaceful rolling sound of water swaying back and forth, to the timeless, continuous song of the great ocean, like the gentle, but powerful flow of steady breathing . . . in and out . . . in and out . . . and let it guide you deeper within to where the vast, unknown virgin spaces of your inner world correspond to the vast, unknown mysterious sea, so full of hidden wonder.

Imagine the panoramas which lie beneath that moving blanket of waves: wide, unexplored landscapes, mountain ranges, valleys, plateaux and plains, jungles of seaweed, rocky deserts — all supporting life in a multitude of climates ranging from cold, subtle and grey in the north and south to warm, lush and dramatically colourful in the regions near the girdle of the earth.

But this diverse, spread-out vastness is all one large connected body of water, a world rich and complete in itself, yet also an interconnected, essential part of nature's whole ecological system. Without the sea our land could not support life; so, too, the realms of our unconscious can seem like a world set apart inside us, full both of danger and promising potential; a world of mysterious inner landscapes largely undiscovered and sometimes hard to access, abounding with vibrant life and unmeasured resources. Yet this world is the fundamental basis of our whole existence. Without the constant nourishment we draw from our unconscious, without the roots growing out of this infinite, all-containing, ever-regenerating, fertile mother soil, our consciousness could not exist, our daily life could not happen.

Just as the greater part of our planet is covered by water and not by land which can be seen and measured in the light of day, so the far greater part of our psyche is unconscious, and like the sea it laps in unceasing waves upon the continents and islands of that which we know, name and understand. Like the shores of new lands emerging from the sea we learn and grow, like land eroding we forget.

Just as all forms of life began in the sea, so our lifeforce and creativity well up from a source deep in our unconscious. And as the sea is immeasurably rich and fertile and has the power to cleanse and renew itself, and to integrate all things, smoothing them down with the help of time, so our unconscious, also, is an unmeasurable realm of potential and inspiration, ever producing new possibilities, never drying up, cleansing and healing all hurts with the help of time. It allows space to live for all those parts of us that find no room on the limited, discriminating, sunlit islands of our conscious reality. Like a huge mother it contains and brings forth all. And just as all water returns to the sea, washing down part of the land, so life, too, must return to the unconscious to rest, to be renewed, and to reunite again with the larger whole. . .

Imagine the abundance of life beneath the surface of waves, so many plants and animals, all different kinds and forms, ranging in size from the minute to the enormous. Tresses of seaweed are wafting this way and that in the currents, tough, rubbery plant forests are clinging on to rocks, and graceful sea-anemones grow along stony shores, responding to the changing tides by closing

FEBRUARY

up or opening out their elegant, flower-like heads of tendrils. Millions of baby fish grow up everywhere in the shallow waters of the shoreline. Crabs and lobsters pick for food amongst the wet vegetation of little pools left by the tide. Among the rocks out at sea, large silent shoals of fish move together as one body. See how they reflect the sunlight coming in through the water like an explosion of silvery sparks. Some fish are of shiny rainbow colours, others a pure silky white speckled with gold, yet others glow with a luminous neon-like colour as if they were lit up from the inside. There are long, slender sea-snakes, translucent jelly-fish, and tiny sea-horses. There are seals and sealions, intelligent dolphins and dangerous sharks, and out in the deep the huge whale moves its powerful body through the wide, cold waters. . .

Take some time to imagine that colourful multitude of shapes, sizes and qualities you can find in the creatures that live in this vast nursery of life, the sea. . . Then let yourself feel what wealth of diversity, strange and wonderful, abounds in the depth of your own inner ocean: unmeasured potential, unknown possibilities, and many a treasure as yet undiscovered.

Now picture the sun shining on the sea: see how the warm golden light tints the clear, grey waters with the subtle colours of the rainbow. Then let that golden glow of sunlight touch the surface of the deep, dark spaces of your own unknown inner world and tint it with a rainbow light.

Take a little while to ponder how much more there is to life than that which we can see and know; and feel the presence of that inner ocean of potential which is always there for you.

Just as the rain that rises from the sea sustains the life of our green earth, creative inspiration welling up from the unconscious is the 'water of life' that can grace your daily awareness with meaning and depth. At times when life seems stale and arid and choice restricted, you might wish to return to your inner shores of spaciousness to look for the distant horizon or sail the rainbow waves from which, quite unexpectedly, some unknown treasure may yet one day be washed ashore. . .